T0109029

WIRE SONG

WIRE SONG

POEMS BY
MARK TODD

WITH A FOREWORD BY
DANA GIOIA

CONUNDRUM

PRESS

Conundrum Press, Crested Butte, Colorado 81224
© 2001 by Mark Todd

All rights reserved. First edition 2001
Printed in the United States of America

05 04 03 02 01   5 4 3 2 1

Cover photograph by Katherine Darrow © 1999

Library of Congress Control Number 2001088635

ISBN 0-9657159-8-1 (pbk.) — ISBN 0-9657159-9-X (cloth)

ACKNOWLEDGMENTS

I wish to thank the editors of the following magazines in which current or earlier versions of some of these poems first appeared: "Night Passages," "River Koan," and "Moon Sister," *Gunnison Valley Journal*; "Early Chores," and "The Doyleville Schoolhouse," *Weber Studies: Contemporary Voices of the West*; "The Bluff," *The Headwaters Reader*.

Several poems appeared in the anthology *The Geography of Hope: Poets of Colorado's Western Slope* (Conundrum Press, 1998), edited by David J. Rothman: "Wire Song," "Son et Lumi`ere," "The Game Trail," "Mud Season," "Rigby," "Grandmother's Farm," and "To Kill Stray Dogs."

Beyond publication credits, I wish to acknowledge several individuals who have contributed variously to the creation of this collection.

More than I can express in the book's dedication, I thank my wife Kym for the continuous encouragement she offered on those many nights when I wanted to share a newly penned poem, and for her patience in allowing me to test on her the countless iterations that most of these pieces subsequently underwent before I could leave them alone.

I also owe an immense debt of gratitude to mentors who have taken the time and trouble to read and to make better many of the poems in this volume. I especially thank Dana Gioia, who showed me ways I could make poetry matter; Keith Wilson, who always insisted that my words could be poems; David Mason, who taught me how to listen to the narrative voice;

George Sibley, who understood the soul of the words; and Robert McDowell, who showed me how to tell a story.

Several of the poems in the current collection benefited from fellow poets John Cope, James Tipton, and Bill King. It was sometimes their advice and sometimes their example that reminded me to keep my lines honest and direct.

Finally, I owe special thanks to David J. Rothman. His support and friendship gave me the courage to persevere, and his insight and skill as an editor helped me to forge these poems into a book.

For Kym,
who understood these poems
before they were words.

CONTENTS

THEN AND NOW

FOREWORD

At the beginning of the twenty-first century America grows ever more homogenous. A childhood in Atlanta is no longer much different from one in Seattle or San Diego. A housing tract built in San Jose looks indistinguishable from one in Cleveland. The same brands of food and clothing are sold from coast to coast. Even regional speech accents are in decline, especially among the social elite. The Internet invites us to dwell—disembodied and placeless—in the World Wide Web of cyberspace. The economic benefits of scale and standardization are more powerful than the less quantifiable losses of local identity and regional character. It is an especially sad irony that nowhere is this standardization more evident than in the arts. Regional music has been homogenized into standard commercial categories by multinational entertainment companies. Local architectural styles hardly exist. Even poetry has become curiously placeless and nomadic as poets crisscross the continent from one writing program or teaching post to another like sophisticated tourists in their own land.

Mark Todd's poetry is a striking exception to this cultural trend. His verse gives memorable expression to a particular place—the high plains and mountain valleys of the Colorado Rockies. There is nothing homespun about his deft and sophisticated work, but it could not have been written anywhere else. Not only his subjects, but his imagery, style, and tone originate in the geography of his home. He is passionately local without ever being parochial, and his work reminds us of how many great poets—Thomas Hardy, Robert Frost, E.A. Robinson, Robinson Jeffers, to name only a few—have purposely situated their verse in a particular place. For them being regional did not mean being provincial. It meant writing vividly from the precise reality of an actual life and landscape.

A careless critic might classify Todd's work as "nature poetry," but that term misapprehends the basic quality of his vision. His poetry portrays a precariously inhabited landscape, which is at once breathtakingly open and harshly unforgiving. His work is pastoral but without the softness that mode usually implies. Todd's perspective is not the urbanite's vision of a simpler country life but an exact and exacting account of what rural life entails. His central subject is the alternately exhilarating and uneasy coexistence of the humanized and inhuman landscape, both the conflict and the concord of rural civilization and wilderness. Todd explores his subject in many ways—the bond between man and animal, the legacy from American Indians to later settlers, the interdependence of country life and local weather. He sets this confrontation and conversation of human consciousness and the natural world in the high mesas and mountains of Colorado, but the drama he depicts is both universal and primal.

One purpose of poetry is to articulate our existence— to give our inchoate experience shape and consciousness so that we might better understand and remember it. No single writer's work can accomplish more than a tiny portion of that ongoing and endless task. What matters is how well it manages. There are so many places in this continent that are still waiting to be storied, to have their essence captured and celebrated by a writer equal to the task. *Wire Song* explores a vast landscape, which it registers for us on a tangible human scale. Todd has written an original and authentic book that opens up new vistas in American poetry. Colorado should welcome this important new poet.

Dana Gioia

WIRE SONG

STANDARDS

No rancher in these parts
Would wear a crease-new hat.
They take special satisfaction
In the weather-chewed
Horse-stomped grease-stained
Feel of fine felt,

The art of it somehow
The measure of any man
Worth his sweat-wrung salt—
A standard I overlooked
For full two years.
And to think, I walked

In broad daylight,
Toting the notion
They admired my brushed
Stetson—Hell,
I'd be a fool to wear it
Out in public now.

But if I sweat the band
And rub the brim enough
With dirt and grease,
One day soon it'll look
The part, as good as any
At a local Sunday social.

MIDNIGHT

Midnight, and a cool breeze
Seeps through the screenless open
Of my window, spreading
The spring smell of pasture grass
Throughout the household.

In a stirless state, awake,
I lie with the sleeping land.

CALVING

Bucking across the rough
pasture, the Jeep's headlamps
pitching from sage to sky:
the night watch, 2 a.m.,
and the vigil of spring,
the wait for newborn calves.

I ride with my neighbor
as he scouts for a sign,
his spotlight tunneling
through dense, huddled shadows,
flashing on wary eyes,
on cross, first-time heifers.

We rock to a sudden
halt, he dashing over
to check on a new birth,
while I nod behind frost
and glass, half-moon dreaming
of my cozy, warm bed.

One by one, two by two,
the numbers multiply
throughout the night, as new life,
slick and fresh, stirs the dark
with cow-calf pairs, ready
for the first feel of dawn.

EARLY CHORES

In the dark, standing, waiting
For the shiver of early chores
To settle bone deep,

The horses, now grained,
Are gray shadows which stand
Against a lifting black.

I watch a crisp, white line
Etch the ragged jaw
Of mountains to the east,

Light soon spilling
Into the valley.
In the pasture, Canadian geese

Take flight, a floating
Phalanx that touches the sunlight
Fingers above our eyes.

They turn
        fly low
                    just overhead.

The horses pause, and together
We watch, waiting our turn
To feel the warmth of light, and day.

ON CATTLE TIME

The drive
Toward town
Feels harried,
But of course,
This is still
Rural Colorado,
And I slow the car:
Now a cautious, driven wedge
Into the herd of cattle
That claims the road,
That readjusts
The schedules
Of spring.

THE DOYLEVILLE SCHOOLHOUSE

squats against foothills,
a tiny solitary block of salt
to the eye that travels
the straight-across mile
from the highway.

Its paint skin, snow-weary
and cracked, tells of years
since anyone learned, or lived
cubbyholed beneath the roof.

But those who live ranch-distant
still feel its rituals—its pie
socials and Halloween apple bobs.

It connects homes too often
separated by calving, haying, by winter
wind and snow-drifted fields.

Some traditions run
deeper than concrete.

This morning the old schoolhouse
wears the full moon like a bonnet,
weathered but proud, and a reminder:

>   the where can sometimes
>   tell us who we are.

GRANDMOTHER'S FARM

The door jamb still stands
Above scorched concrete, above
A charred collapse of planks—
All that's left
Of Grandmother's house.

A propane leak, they said,
Too far from town
For firefighters, too old
And weathered to save.

My cousin and uncle
Later torched the rest,
The blaze driving out
Scores of rats
From corn crib and barn.
Their soot-smeared bodies
Charcoaled the winter ground
With lines of retreat:

Target practice
Under a frozen,
Panhandle sky.

A day when snow mingled
With ash and blood.

THE BIRTHDAY

A .22 was all it took,
and a rifle caressed
by proud hands once ranch
rough—hands that now wore
the brittle of decay,
trapped most days by bed
clothes, or pressed hard
against smooth walls.

But this day, sitting
in his son's pick-up,
promised for rabbit hunting,
he sat alone.

And while his son
fetched the old man's
hat inside, no one
heard the pop, or saw him
slump, a burgundy trickle
seeping from his chin,
painting the hound's-tooth
checkers on his shirt.

El Niño

It's been a black-bale summer,
Cubes of hay rained to a dull gray,
Lying like fossils beside tracks
Of stubbled stalk. Already

Fall smiles its aspen streaks
Across the mountainside, mocking
The valley floor with fall's unkempt
Harvest of flotsam, golden leaves.

But on a late September day,
Nearby rakes and balers stand
Silent in the mud of the field,
Their behemoth bodies at rest

As they sleep like sluggish beasts
And dream of drier summers.
The clouds frown at the afternoon,
And their dark bellies open:

Trickles of water soon sheet
Across the window pane, blurring
The pasture, rain pounding
Against the skin of the world.

Mud Season

Tires chew into the soft,
April earth, drop easily
into ruts that sluice
the passages of spring
through country roads.

The fields still linger
with five months' snowwash,
stock trails crisscrossing
the meadow-white. No longer
content with aging bales,

the horses search, paw
at the crust thaw, hungering
for the shootgreen grass
that surely lies beneath.
Across the pasture

I ease the truck
toward their gate,
a weary struggle
against mud channels
that later will lead to home.

Rain

When I awake at dawn,
Your fingertip droplets
Trill ever so lightly
Along my rooftop line.
You rub careless streamlets
Down the posts that stanchion
What's left of the resolve
Of my deck against you.
I gaze into your lies,
Your cloud-dark eyes and wet
Breath, so scented and musked,
A promiscuous game
Of desire.
       But I, lulled
And drowsed by your whispered
Promises, will arise
Too late to discover
You've sauntered down meadow,
That there you'll share your charms
With others, leaving me
Breath-shallowed.
          So go on.
I'll wait here, languish here
For your sprinkling lisp, your
Laugh,
      and then I'll follow,
Gladly taking the terms
Of your making, licking
Your trifling wet favors,
Best when I know others
Are gaping with envy.

13

CHINKS

Under a pelt of chinks,
Strapped on tight as stretched skin,
The fit's like a cinched hug,
And leathery—the edged
Cut fingers of long fringe

Strumming against your legs.
The feel just readies you
To rub the world's brambles,
Cow hide laughing at thorns,
At everyday thistle.

WIRE SONG

The country here-abouts
Can be told best in wire.

It's a history that's spun
In ways books seldom bind,
In ways where the knowing
Of this land's recounted
In strands with barbs for bards.

Wire stories our telling
By twisting those legends
Of posts smacked split-rock hard,
Pounded and then sturdied,
Wedged with flint and talus.

Wire can plot straights of line
Through boundaried stretches
Over ground that's broken
With ditch and arroyo.

It smoothes the sense of harsh
And unforgiving land,
The stumble through pastured
Grasses fed by stone-fast
Roots, by tangles of brush.

Taut and strong in the wind,
Wire strings tales from steel yarn,
Singing the lines of place
Through rusted, untold words.

STOMP AND BRONC WAYS

THE FOAL

The down-up-down, then up
Told us the time had come:
So close, this first-time mare.
But she not yet bagged up
And unready, early
For a spring cold snap foal.

Still, there was no doubt now.
With her water breaking,
I quick barn-led tugged her.
She dropped to the stall floor
And pushed out the white sack
Of head, then stopped to breathe.

I gouged a finger tear
Around the tiny mouth—
Anything to give it
A chance to draw a breath—
When she heaved out the rest
On bedding of thrown straw.

It lay quiet, and still,
As we pulled the sheathing
Of afterbirth away.
We watched with wrenched-tight hearts:
Mare nuzzling tiny hooves,
Urging some show of life.

. . . So we carried it off,
Leaving her in the stall
With the foal's stained imprint
On birth-blood empty straw.

Farrier Day

i

It's come farrier day
that the routine of things
can go beat-skip stumbling
past the expected ruts—
something only horses
can feel the measure of.
Soon their heads are brush-thrust,
thicket-thick in the hope
I'll not see their bodies
if all eyes lie hidden.

ii

But (horses caught and tied)
the humiliation
feels keenest when cow dogs
circle for the hoof feast,
darting under bellies
to snatch up fresh trimmings,
paw-clutching their morsels,
soft crescents they can squeeze
against the open hinge
of jaws and fast-smacked lips.

iii

The horses stand and pout,
resigned to live a stock
life that offers not one
a promised graze-long day.
The temper of steel shoes
bothers less their feet than
sultry dispositions.
But stamp-fuss and tantrum
turn quiet when flat files
pop the dance from their rumps.

iv

They endure the hammer
that tap-fits new foot wear
and brings a settled stance.
Then, at last, each in turn
is loosed back to pasture,
and the herd can gather,
readjust to freedom.
They single-file their way,
tunnel sockets through trees,
feel safe, for now, again.

HALTER BREAKING

Weanling filly, and slick
As sweat, champing her lips
In fear at the blunt rude
Very bother of me.
Still, I manhandle head
Fit to halter, I watch
Muscle quiver her side.

This inelegant dance
Blunders into a sort
Of horse-and-man two-step,
She tilting on pegged hooves,
Teetering against arms
That hold her tight, a clamp
To make her surrender.

The solution is this:
Natural unwilling
So separates the wild
Of this horse from man-tame,
I must insist that she
Gentle, that she quiet
To the hand of my touch.

RIGBY

It was the time that Rigby
(Sixteen hands so bay and shiny)
First saw cattle.
Seven years old but still box-stall baby.
Ears quivering to hooves,
Caprioling over bunch grass,
Not knowing that heifers,
All doe-eyed and curious,
Would not thunder their numbers
Through barbed wire and get him.

Rigby
      bringing to pasture a schooling
      of groomed earth, of race track,
And me
      his gentrified, unschooled equal—

How comical we must have seemed
To ranch neighbors, polite but smiling,
As they watched us both that summer day
While we tried to walk a country road.

A Horse Named Habit

You bet a Habit
Is hard to break,
You tall-standing
Son of a bitch.
I still gimp
From your knee-bust
Stomp and bronc ways,
A hit-hard lesson.
And to see you still
Too-grained full
Of yourself
While I feel only
The punched-breath
Crunch of flat
Pack and trail.
But I'll find the cool
Of your blood yet
Between my knees,
The settle-down
Of your gait,
The steady
Of quieter days.

BULL RIDER

So restless to ride, rough stock in his blood,
As he climbs atop the tall fencing rails.

It's a chute stuffed 2,000 pounds full
Of a mad, bull-twisting kind of mean.
But still the rider bends stiff legs
Down inside the stall, squeezes against the sides
Of a muscle-monster they call Scorched Heat.

A cowboy-crazy sort of thing to do:
He grips the leather braids and starts to pound
Each of his gloved fingers tight into place,
Snugging his thighs and crotch behind the hump,
Hoping his luck'll be better than his draw.
He nods and the gate flings open to eject

Bull-rider together, briefly partnered
To spin side-winding clockwise in mid-air.
Then a piston-slam from the massive head,
So quick that it cold-cocks the luckless rider,
His body rag-doll falling to soft dirt,
Never hearing the spectators' Oohs! Aahs!
Or the matter-of-fact announcer's voice
Bouncing off the stands with "That's gotta hurt."

But he'll be back—if he can just get up.
Still restless to ride, rough stock in his blood.

High Country Ride

The clip of pony feet—the only sound
That bonds the spirit of our trek to bone,
That brings the anchored feel of rock and ground.

We climb up past the trees where skies surround
The peaks with silence, and alone
The clip of pony feet—the only sound.

A ridgeline trail spills vistas all around.
Beneath our feet the sturdiness of stone
Brings back the anchored feel of rock and ground.

Swirled mists of early evening gray resound
And then they echo back the steady tone
And clip of pony feet—the only sound.

Through jut and crag we pick our way back down.
We cannot always live up high, alone
To sense the anchored feel of rock and ground.

These moments bring the lost in us to found.
It's only for a moment we can own
The clip of pony feet—the only sound
That brings this anchored feel of rock and ground.

COMMON GROUND

NIGHT PASSAGE

A twilight drive, just up ahead
The last few strays of light had fixed
Their glow against a rim of rock
Before the valley plunged into night.

A ribbon of road led me home
As headlamps pushed against the dim,
A feel of shrinking space that closed
Behind my car and soon reduced

The future to a hundred feet,
Advancing slowly, as though beams
Could somehow thaw the gravel road,
Or thaw the winter yet to come—

Then suddenly, a moving wall
Began to block my journey home.
The darkened silhouettes of elk,
A herd of fifty—maybe more—

That cluster-ran across the road,
The ragged top-line of the group
An upward thrusting rack of heads
Above the mass of their band-bulk.

And as I passed their crossing point,
I stopped, listened as pumping lungs
Heaved billows into frosted breath,
Unseen in the black, moonless night.

ECLIPSE

I couldn't tell you the numbered times I've seen
The moon's arc, its flat medallion a traced
Path across the canopy-sky, its face
In two dimensions, like a spotlight-beam;
Or the thoughtless times I've assumed that its scheme
Of things was merely a bright plate that effaced
The stars, a celestial disk too long encased
In the time-weary lines of a lover's theme.

But that still night, when the earth's shadow licked
Away the moon's full milk-veneer, I stood
On the dark deck, and through a reddish trick
Of light, it seemed a suspended world I could
Almost touch, suddenly a solid place,
A sphere that hung in the deep room of space.

SON ET LUMIÈRE

It's in the featureless
Lay of the great High Plains
That heads of anvilled storm
Vault full-afternoon blown,
That the flat face of land
Brushes sky into gust-
Borne scenery, that new-
Born, free-form horizons
Can merge a somehow ground
With the fastened texture
Of a darkening thunder,
With those lightning-stroke sparks
Through glimpsed-fire discharges,
An almost living thing,
Heavy with the weightless,
Touchless push of a breath
That closes southwest days.

Flat Country

Horizon so flat that even a tree
Catches your eye, spilling the land
Freely and full of an easy flow.
The plains open wide to the heart

And sprawl out far as you can feel.
Their sight pummels your breast bare
And wicks up your spine with wonder
At the skyline, down flush, and low.

This is the floor of the world, fusing
Sand to clinging roots, pressing
Hard on cracked soil, on the skin
Of life, stretched tight in the heat.

The earth waits for a flashing flood
To wash the vast scope of things,
To put order to the land's lay,
To its settle, silence, and sweep.

THE GAME TRAIL

There! She says, and sure
Enough, up the gouge
Of Barret Creek, the soft
Honk-like calls of cow elk
To calves, their great tan
And white bulk speckled
With the shadowcast of aspen.
We work uphill, upwind
Over sage and talus,
Over a trail made by game,
My stepdaughter scrambling
Ahead, I trying to close ranks.
I stumble often in this uneasy
Journey, one that reaches
Past today's late afternoon sun.
I know the tug of thread
Between us often snaps,
And I lose the way connecting
Our paths, we both standing
Distantly, side by side.
But there are moments,
Like today, when we surprise
Ourselves surprising elk,
Face to face in a stumbled-on
Clearing of common ground.

THE OUTDOORS

The outdoors I like best
comes easily enough:
splashed face-straight with both hands
cupped full of creek water
after a day's long mend
to troubled sags of fence,
or stooped against the bank
when I pry sweat-stuck boots
from grateful feet, from toes
flexing at cramped contours—
a feeling all spangled
in mute-shouted stretch-joy.

The outdoors I like best
can shove me into walks
along moist, edged shadows,
a sweet pungent decay
chattering on and on
about life grown from death,
singing through scents and shade.
The outdoors I like best
springs up, an unaware
moment, unforgotten,
so lingering it still
bends me back to a smile.

Moon Sister

Summer clouds talon the full moon,
Stretch wings across the night
That whisper to a feathered sister below,
To eyes that sweep the dark.
There's an unseen clutch,
A drama without malice,
But unrelenting nonetheless.
So unforgiving,
This triumph cloaked by moon
Both silvered and shadowed.

ROAD CREW

A raven's down-sweep up and thrust
To reach the strands of fence-top wire,
Rattled by snow-crunching crust
In the hum-come of road to tire.

Then a swoop-land savor and delight,
The relish of pecked meat in the sun,
A frenzy of carcass claw and fright
As the hop-close dissection's begun.

A flock-so-feisty crew, well honed
For scavenge-perfect chaos, devised
To undo skew-clattering bone,
The dwindle of flesh in caws and cries.

They hunger, watch on a roadside slope.
They wait for a same-ending way:
Skid marks lead to a carrion's hope,
But they seldom lead to decay.

RIVER KOAN

for T.L.

I slip a wooden paddle
Into the weave of the current,
Caressing the river
With the language of my hands,
With strokes that sound out
Liquid syllables, that resonate
Deep inside my chord-core.
My hands are tongues,
Intoning with something closer
Than other, a feel
Both guide and guided,
A surrender to the tug
Of siren call and flow,
A channel of water-kin
Self through a water-soft breath,
Commingling with the *a capella*
Voices that chant the push
And pull of the river.

PASSAGES

Layers of mesa sink
Into the blues of soft
Twilight, into the shades
That hide the sundown halt
Of two gypsy wagons,
Camping by the roadside.

Their burros graze deeply
The lush ditch of nearby
Ojo Caliente,
Where a night's rest passes
Unremarked in a land
Scribed by the ruts and signs
Of road-weary travel.

These back-road passages
Still guide lost wanderers,
No matter the distance
Of the journey called home.

THE STAND

Does wind feel fresh to swaying trees,
Their up-most branches out of sight,
Their push against a bending breeze,
Their fin-thin limbs like tethered kites?

An uplift, timbered, sighing hush
Gives silent stands a thankful voice
That balances the wind's smooth rush
And pumps their limbs to guide the moist

Which flows up from the roots below,
To feed the trunks with sap and force,
A constant ebb, a constant flow,
To match the seasons' change of course.

Who knows how wood can feel the wind?
We only know what we can see:
The pushing breeze, the swaying trees,
The needled fins' whirl, glide, and bend.

TOMICHI DOME

We sat on the deck,
Tomichi Dome bulking
Dark before us,
Its talused Buffalo
Face thrust bluntly,
Filling the landscape
With a shaggy hump
Of rock and tree.

Beams danced skyward
Above its mass—
The Northern Lights.
I slipped my hand
In yours as we watched
In silence, partners
Under the vast, playful
Screen of the night.

TUMIT CHE:

           words in Ute
that mean "mountain stream."
It's the headwater-trickle
through tundra, a cascade,
a passage that wears rock
with time and flow.

It's the liquid rush cobbling
pebbles into the bed
of a creek, and the scrawl
of horns and oxbows
to cross a narrow plain
shouldered by hills.

These days we say "Tomichi,"
affixed to roads, signs,
even storefront names,
but somehow too distant
from the water or land.
Tumit Che names more,

more than store or sign.
Through tundra, stream,
rock and plain,
Tumit Che names this place,
its sense, and more—
our belonging.

41

THE DREAM CATCHER

On a fine
June morning,
the elders
from three
Council Fires
gather, speak
in turn
their thoughts
on things
much larger
than this shanty room.
Then silence,
while all eyes
follow the spider
picking its way
across the bare floor.
A good omen,
which no one
mentions.

THE THREE SISTERS

The eyes just turn that way:
Travelling on up-slope,
Far past the stream's trickle,
Where fraying willow roots
Suck at snow-melt run-off.

Up higher still, to watch
The three volcanic necks,
Their pillars jutting up
High above spruce and fir,
Their fire-tempered rock plugs

A stanchion to the sag
And bloat of summer clouds.
Like hags frozen in dance,
Their chant of stone pulls down
The thunder, the rumble,

The crack of sparked daggers
And the rain's sudden fall
In misted, silent sheafs,
Hiding sheer mass and rock
In dark, drenching showers.

Two Worlds

A vast shell half-clouds
Midday sky, weightlessly
Pressing snow fields
Into sheets of gray.

Shadows, skirting daylight,
Wrap the cold, they hold
Winter's settle deep
In the frozen ground.

But the sun spreads
Across the other half-world
Above me. Light splinters
Through branches, casts splotches

Of warmth across my jeans
As I, on the chopped head
Of a stump, and grateful,
Sit, waiting for spring.

THEN AND NOW

COYOTES

The summer chill—I still remember that—
And then the careless, quick and eager chase
Of our young yearling Lab, her lion heart
Ready to charge across the open field.
The rounded moon beamed bright as daylight
And glanced flat off a single silhouette,
Motionless in the pasture, lonely and dark,
Chattering, teasing, luring our Lab along,
Calling her out.   Her broad paws hammered
Through foot-high grass, cutting a broken path
Toward that wail, that voice thrust at the sky,
A voice as plaintive as any child's could be.
But when our dog approached, the figure turned,
Retreated several steps: its stacatto
Of quieter yips still coaxing the Lab on,
And always farther from our "Come!" commands.
Only then did we see the other three emerge,
Like shouldered heads that sprouted from the grass.

Our Lab stopped short, her nose stretched up and out,
And though uncertain of her ground, she faced,
In turn, the trotting members of the pack,
Tried to stand them off, to fight them one on one.
It was almost a dance, or a ritual,
Rehearsed in the blood of countless other kills.
They circled in around her, like drawstrings
That tightened the arcs of the hunt—no escape
For their victim, whose snarls began to edge with fear.

A neighbor told us once, the year before,
How he'd come one time along a road,
How he'd seen them, gathered in the ditch,
The cow frantic, and the way they'd dragged
Her calf, a newborn, past the wire-strand fence
To tear at the meat, soft, tender, living.
He'd fired into the pack, the spray of bullets
Never finding a true mark, but barking
Loud enough to make them scurry off.

I raced into the house and grabbed a gun,
An old revolver hardly worth the point
And shoot at such a range, but squeezed off rounds
That emptied all six chambers.
But all at once, that somehow did the trick,
And one by one, they melted, though unhurried,
Into the tall reeds of the moon-gray grass.
So our young dog, bounding toward the house,
Found the chance to make her way back, lucky,
And with her tail now tucked between her legs.

That week, we heard their coming back again.
We listened, the plead and yearn of their far calls
Magnified by a pall of evening mist.
We could sense their prowl, an ever-stalking presence
That returned, restless to finish the hunt.
Our Lab lay still, a moan-like growl swelling
Her throat, but her form hugged the side of the house.
She hackled at their vigilance,
Their certain watch past bright light's ragged edge.

To Kill Stray Dogs

Stomping to the house
a mile-away neighbor
lets the mad of his .30-06
point straight at our dogs.

Seems he's found five
calves, bone-licked clean,
their lipless baby teeth
grimacing at the dull sky
of winter. Not enough
leftover flesh and hide
for coyote work, he says,
knowing full well it's
our dogs live closest by.

But we've seen the pack
whose hunger could run down
the fall size of spring heifers.
Not two days before, three
dogs chased our daughter's pick-up,
as if a pick-up could rescue
the lost from their eyes.

But now their tongues
too much taste the salt
of fresh kill—they'll get
no stockgrower's pity. Now,
I, too, must harden
the dog-soft of my heart
(or I may wake one night

to snarls that tear at the legs
of our weanling filly), must go
with the party that will hunt
them from the valley . . .

   Tonight my head shifts,
turns upon a comfortless bed.
My dreams search the hills
and drainages to the east
of our place, restless until
they see the three dark forms:
forms that lie still, silent
under the huddle and gray
of a splash-cold moon.

Marshall Pass

Big Jim Vernon was moving cows
Up the road to Marshall Pass,
A trip he'd made for forty years,
But a trip that was never fast.

Just him, his horse, and a dog called Scratch
To push the herd up high,
To get what good they could of grass
Where mountains meet on sky.

The dog would circle back around
And give the strays a nip,
While Jim would wave and slap his rope
Or call out with a yip.

He punched the cows and calves along
All spread from ditch to ditch.
They'd maybe gone a dozen miles
Without a single hitch.

Old Scratch, it was, first heard the noise,
A motor's whining drone
That interrupted any calm
From riding trail alone.

Jim watched the motorcycle's pace,
Its rider all ablaze
In reddish helmet, bib and gloves
Beneath the dust and haze.

Jim's horse had mostly seen it all,
From lightning storms to bears,
But still she shied and tossed her head,
Her nostrils wide and flared.

He checked the startled, anxious cows
And settled down his horse.
He waved his rope to slow the bike,
Whose roar was loud and coarse.

"I'd take it kindly if you'd wait,"
Jim tried to speak his say.
"Just let me move the cows aside
And you'll be on your way."

The stranger tapped his helmet's side
And then he shook his head.
The engine's roar had drowned Jim's voice.
The bike gunned on ahead.

Jim only knew he had to act,
For he had no desire
To doctor all those baby calves
Who'd spook near roadside wire.

He trotted up beside the bike
And gave his horse a boot.
They jumped in front and stopped it cold,
Then reined up with a scoot.

The biker shook an angry fist,
Then revved his engine up.
He started, once again, to pass,
But Jim had had enough.

He flipped his rope to make a loop
And twirled his ready lasso,
Then flung the rope to drop straight down
And snag that biker yahoo.

Jim passed the rope by the saddle horn
And dallied twice around,
Then leaned back hard to feel the tug
That plucked the biker down.

The rider, he looked mad as hell
But made no move to fight
When Scratch began to snarl and growl
And looked like he would bite.

The bike slid down and flooded out
Before it reached the herd.
So Jim, still mounted, sauntered up
To have a final word.

"Pardner, I'll bet you take it slow
When you run into rock.
You need to take it slower though
When you ride up on stock."

Jim didn't waste another word,
Just let it go at that.
He turned to punch his cows along
And left the stranger flat.

Now, if you drive up Marshall Pass
You'd best be looking out
For Jim and his herd along the road,
Or else, find another route.

THE BLUFF

Ned Delaney settled his rhythm to work,
Letting the fall of his post-hole digger
Cut into the cracked, crusted earth.
The monotony of hammered strokes pushed
Ned's thoughts past the day's labor
And his day-dream self sat,
Boot propped, on a tall bar stool,
An hour in the sun no longer long
When he thought of Belinda tending bar,
Her blue-eyed gaze as strong as any beer.

Which might explain why Ned would not have seen
The pick-up's approach, its winding climb
To where he worked, to where he dreamed the end
Of a hot day that might lead to love,
Or at least the look of that bartending beauty.

And which might explain why Ned didn't care
To waste words on the likes of Cutthroat Mueller,
Who by then, bumping to a rough stop,
Let fling through the open pick-up door
A long string of chopped, hard words.

Ned shook his head sharply left to right,
Separating the dream-feed of his thoughts
From the curled lip and threat of Mueller's shouts.
Though the tirade came mostly in German,
Ned guessed the tone's intent all right:

- Get off my land—und take your fence!

Ned had been warned about old Cutthroat,
Nicknamed not for a love of trout,
But for darker, much darker reasons.
Ned returned the stare-down glare.

- Survey shows your land stops—

Mueller cut in with broken English,

- You have no right! I lease this land!

- May be. I just work
  Where they tell me. You got a beef,
  Talk to the BLM.

Old Man Mueller wasn't buying it,
And true, there seemed no reason for the fence.
Still, Ned turned back to the job at hand,
Raised and chunked the double-bladed spade
Down to hollow out a deeper socket.
It was then he heard the click-catch of the cock,
And looked up to see Mueller's gun
Thirty yards away, trained on his chest.

- Clear out, or I shoot!

The bite of work sweat stung Ned's eyes,
As he let the wooden handles of the digger fall.
He reached for his neck-slung bandana
And wiped his face.

Then he walked to his truck.
A job nearly done—and so close
To heading back to look for Belinda's smile.

He pulled his rifle from the back window rack.
In two beats of his heart, he spread-eagled
Beside the truck, stretched half-across
The hood, elbow propping the leveled gun,
And drew a steady bead dead center
At old Mueller's opening wide eyes.

- Better make your shot count.

A breeze stiffened the distance between the two,
And neither man seemed able to move
Until Mueller began to hack and cough.
A bloated humph! filled his puffy cheeks.

- You are too rash, my friend.
You do not value life enough.

Mueller let the weight of his barrel drop,
In three relaxing jerks, to rest on the ground.

- I got no time to waste on you.

But Mueller's voice had lost its sharp edge,
And he backed into his pick-up,
Shouting through the half-closed window,

56

- This is not the end, young friend!

Ned only nodded once, slowly,
As the small bead at the end of his rifle followed
The old man's retreat down the road.
Ned released his held breath and turned
Again to the new row of fence posts . . .

But Mueller, he never bothered Ned again,
Though Ned kept the rifle close at hand,
And just as it had been that day:
unloaded.

Little Arkansas

Prologue

"It was, of course, a wilder world back then,"
She said, and leaned back in her chair.
A hundred years, and more, of family tales
Now separated early times from mine,
The times my mother's mother knew his name:
Her cousin, Wes—but called John Wesley Hardin.
She was just a child when family said
He was the meanest man she'd ever know,
A Texas desperado, and wanted then
For killing scores of men. Loyal to some,
But murderous still by all accounts.
But all accounts had never told the tale,
"The time he rode beside his cousin, Jim,
The time a younger Wes first earned the name
Of Little Arkansas," her voice began.

i

The drovers, gathered round about the fire,
Wore faces streaked with light, reddened darkly
By the glow, but wearing admiration
All the same—a sight that sickened Jim.
They hung on Wes's every word.

"Those six vaqueros
Should've known, trespassing every one,
And when they pushed me, why, I had no choice.
The steers were ours."
                              "So what'd you do?"
"Why, I charged right in, and shot 'em dead."
"All six?"
                    "Hell no, my cousin, here, nailed one."

Jim shivered at his part, and even more
At Wes's easy telling of the lie.

"Of course, I got the rest myself, just dropped
My reins and spurred on in. I let 'em feel
The taste of both my .45s, I did."

But, by now, it was just too late to tell,
The truth, that is, of what they'd really done.
Besides, the Chisholm Trail was reckless and full
Of regret. Now near the end, no turning back
Could undo the blood they'd shed, or undig
Those mounds beside the Little Arkansas.

By tomorrow's end, they'd bring in the herd
To Abilene, a sort of sprung-up town
To mark the end of cattle drives.

                                        Jim saw
The chance and splashed his coffee and the grounds
At the fire, a hiss and spit that said enough,
Without the need of words, to scatter the group
And send each weary member to his bed.

A hand against his cousin's arm, Jim spoke,
"Wes, we need to talk."
                              "That name don't suit me.
The others call me Little Arkansas."
"Wes, we need to talk—not of foolish names,
But of what you'll do in Abilene. There's talk—"
"—You mean about the showdown."
                                        "Yes, there's that.
But Wes, don't let it come to that, to blood."

Jim could see his cousin's outline, the change
In how he stood, under the stars, the change
In his voice, not of his only eighteen years.
Wes was so swallowed by pride, like a snake
Around a mouse, that Jim could hardly see
A boy at all, hardened where he sat.
But the change had come when Wes had shot and killed
The men beside the Little Arkansas.
Jim had fired in self defense when the fight,
Blown hot and full by Wes's words, began.
But Wes had shot the final two, hands raised
And calling it quits—not that Jim would tell,
Bound by blood and kin, by family honor.

"Wes, let's go to town, we'll drink and play cards,
And then let's leave, let's head back home."

Wes shrugged and said, "Whatever you say."
But Jim already knew, no doubting now
That Wes would do, strong-willed, what Wes would do.

ii

It was the other drovers' fault, perhaps.
Their taunt was like coyotes, trying to spook
The younger steers, to startle them to run.
"You can do it, Little Arkansas," they'd told him,
"You're twice as fast." Twice as dangerous,
          thought Jim,
And cool heads, not fast hands, would walk away.
"You'll put my cousin in a box!" he'd shouted,
But they'd circled back around, they'd talked to Wes
Behind his back, sure Wes could beat Hickok,
A seasoned gun, and law in Abilene.

When they rode into town, they saw the sign
To leave all guns outside. Jim glanced at Wes,
Who only winked, and spurred his horse ahead.
Jim followed close behind his cousin's shout,
"I've heard tell of that place,"
                              and soon reined up
At the Alamo Saloon.

                              "Let's have a drink,
And play those cards, I'm feelin' kinda lucky."
"We'll play, and then we'll leave. We'll head on back
For home."
                        "Whatever you say." That wink again.
Not quite sincere, more like a horse, not honest,
Waiting, wanting its rider to relax
Deep into the saddle, before the buck.
That would be Wes, pitching to Kingdom Come.

Jim was settled in a chair, from weariness,
When Hickok showed, but Jim was quick to note
The careful narrow of Hickok's gaze, down
To the handles of Wes's twin .45s.
There was nothing Jim could do but watch
Hickok striding across the room to stand
Before the boy.

                        "I reckon you'd be the one
They're calling Arkansas."
                              "That'd be me.
And you'd be Heykok."
                              "I'll be taking those."
Hickok's glance on the guns again.
                                    "Would you?"

Jim stepped closer to Wes, and placed his hand
On Wes's shoulder, who, for a third time
That day gave him a wink, and a nod.

"Don't even try it, boy. Pass me those guns
Butt-first, nice and easy."

                              Jim heaved a sigh
And stepped away: late, just too damn late to stop
The blood.

                  "Whatever you say, Heykok, sir."

Don't do it.

                  Wes slowly began to pull
His pistols, butt-first, from his belt, easy
From his holsters, and raised his arms out straight.

Not to him, don't do it, thought Jim, *not this,*
Not to him, but the thought had barely crossed,
Barely formed in Jim's mind, when Wes wrist-flicked
And rolled the guns over, thumbs catching cocks
And pointing both barrels at Hickok's face.

Jim watched the marshal's eyes, unrippled and cool
As blue-gray water, but he let his mouth
Wrinkle warily to smile.

                    "You've got pluck,
I'll give you that. Son, you've got me wrong.
It's not me, the one who's looking for trouble.
Holster those guns and let's talk just a might,
And, maybe, I'll give you a bit of advice."

Jim fought the need to slap his cousin, hard
And full across the face, but he didn't,
He didn't even look back as he walked
Across the floor, through the door, to his horse.

iii

It was hours before the others arrived.
One, Jim could never remember his name,
But one even younger than Wes, came up
And started to gab.
                    "You should've seen it!
Arkansas just sitting there, playing cards
With Heykok hisself. You should've seen it!"
"I've seen enough."
                    "You're not saddling to go?"
"I've had enough. Tell Wes . . . I've had enough.
If he comes back, you tell him that I've gone.
Tell him that I've left for home, and he should do
The same."

            But Jim knew that Wes would never come,
Not home, no, he would not come home again.

EPILOGUE

My mother's mother's voice was silent then,
Her eyelids wrinkled with the years, and closed,
Dreaming deep into a world I'd never know.
She'd made no lesson of her family tale,
And maybe just a story meant to please,
A family tale of cousins now long dead.

But still I couldn't help, I had to ask
About the time she'd said I had his look.
Her eyes still closed, she answered quietly,
"His look? I guess you do—you've got his blood,
Just never let it make you turn away."
From home, I knew she meant.

                              Though now I live
A thousand miles away, and seldom make
The visit back. I never seem to find
The time these days, and even if I think
I'll call, I don't.
                    I guess it's in the blood,
This westering, this loneliness, this song.